Mary Lowe Dickinson

Edelweiss: an Alpine Rhyme

Mary Lowe Dickinson

Edelweiss: an Alpine Rhyme

ISBN/EAN: 9783743301054

Hergestellt in Europa, USA, Kanada, Australien, Japan

Cover: Foto ©Thomas Meinert / pixelio.de

Manufactured and distributed by brebook publishing software
(www.brebook.com)

Mary Lowe Dickinson

Edelweiss: an Alpine Rhyme

EDELWEISS

AN ALPINE RHYME

BY

MARY LOWE DICKINSON

NEW YORK

1876

In memory of the loving kindness that has welcomed them one by one, the author dedicates these verses to the friends at whose request they have been gathered together.

CONTENTS.

6　CONTENTS.

I.

EDELWEISS.

BY Alpine road, beneath an old fir tree,
　　Two children waited patiently for hours;
One slept, and then the elder on her knee
　　Made place for baby head among her flowers.

And to the strangers climbing tired and slow,
　　She called, "Buy roses, please," in accents mild,
As if she feared the echo, soft and low,
　　Of her own voice might wake the sleeping child.

And many came and passed, and answered not
　　The pleading of that young uplifted face,
While, in each loiterer's memory of the spot,
　　Dwelt this fair picture full of patient grace.

And one took offered flowers with gentle hand,
 And met with kindly glance the timid eyes,
And said, in tones that children understand,
 " My little girl, have you the Edelweiss ? "

II.

" Oh, not to-day, dear lady," said the child.
 " I cannot leave my little sister long ;
I cannot carry her across the wild ;
 She grows large faster than my arms grow strong.

" If you stay on the mountain all the night,
 At morning I will run across the steep,
And get the mossy flowers ere sun is bright,
 And while my baby still is fast asleep."

" Your baby, little one ? " " Oh, yes," she said.
 " Yonder, you see that old stone tower shine ?
There, in the church-yard, lies my mother, dead,
 And since she died the baby has been mine."

Soft shone the lady's eyes with tender mist,
   And ever, as' she pressed toward fields of ice,
She pondered in her heart the half-made tryst
   With this young seeker of the Edelweiss.

III.

At night, safe sheltered in the convent's fold,
   Where white peaks stand in ermined majesty ;
Where sunsets pour great throbbing waves of gold
   Across the white caps of a mountain sea.

At morn, with face subdued and reverent tone,
   Slow winding down, with spirit hushed and awed,
As from a vision of the great white throne,
   Or vail half lifted from the face of God.

The blessing of the hills her soul had caught
   Made all the mountain-track a path of prayer,
Along which angel forms of loving thought
   Led to the trysting-place ;—no child was there !

The wind was moaning in the old fir tree,
   The lizards crawling o'er the mossy seat ;
But no fair child, with baby at her knee,
   And in the mold no track of little feet.

IV.

No faded flowers strewing the stunted grass ;
   No young voice singing clear its woodland strain ;
No brown eyes lifted as the strangers pass ;
   A murmur in the air, like far-off rain ;

A black-cloud, creeping downward swift and still,
   Answered her listening heart, a far-off knell,
Almost before there swept along the hill
   The slow, deep tolling of the valley bell.

Once more there drifted 'cross the face the mist ;
   Once more, with trembling soul and tender eyes,
She hurried on to keep the half-made tryst,
   To meet the child, to claim the Edelweiss.

Nearer she came and nearer every hour,
    Her heart-beat answering quick the deep bell's call ;
It led her to the shadow of the tower,
    The shining tower beside the church-yard wall.

v.

She found her there—a cross rose at her feet,
    And burning tapers glimmered at her head;
Her white hands clinging still to blossoms sweet,
    And God's peace on her face ; the child was dead !

Quaint carven saints and martyrs stood around.
    Each clasped the symbol of his sacrifice ;
But this fair child, in saintly sweetness crowned,
    Held, as they held the cross, her Edelweiss.

Early that morn a shepherd, on the height,
    In cleft of rocks sought shelter from the cold,
And there he found this lamb, all still and white,
    Entered already to the heavenly fold.

The Edelweiss grew on that rocky steep ;
The brave child-feet had climbed too fast and far ;
And so had come to her this blessed sleep,
This blessed waking 'neath the morning star.

VI.

The light within the little church grew dim,
And, ere the last gleam faded in the west,
While childish voices sang the vesper hymn,
A lady, with a babe upon her breast,

Crept silently adown the shadowy aisle,
And, kneeling, bathed with tears the hand of ice,
And laid it on the babe, and saw it smile,
And whispered, " I have named her Edelweiss ! "

———

When one more day had seen its shadows fall,
That old stone tower gleaming in the sun,
And the great olive by the western wall,
Shaded two humble graves where had been one.

And by and by, above the dear child's head,
  Arose a little stone with quaint device.
When summer blossoms died around the bed,
  A marble hand grasped still the Edelweiss.

II.

THANKSGIVING.

TRUE I have lost my treasures ; yet to-day
I cannot, grieving, pray,
Mourning the joys of which I am bereft.
I lift mine eyelids up, instead, and say :
Behold how much is left.

Still soft along the sky the white clouds run ;
Still shines the blessed sun ;
Still voice of running water greets my ear ;
Still cross my twilights stars gleam one by one,
And I can see and hear—

Can see the warm light on the shaded ways,
Can hear the birds' sweet praise,
And oft the wayward wind among the leaves,
And the low drip of rain in clouded days
Upon my cottage eaves.

So, while summer blossoms clothe the ground,
    Or falls the happy sound
Of little children's voices in the air,
I still shall find the world with sweetness crowned,
    And comfort everywhere ;

Still find a grateful song for moans of pain,
    A gentle triumph strain,
To calm the sadness of my halting verse.
Under each seeming loss a certain gain ;
    A blessing in each curse.

III.

IF WE HAD BUT A DAY.

WE should fill the hours with the sweetest things,
  If we had but a day;
We should drink alone at the purest springs
  In our upward way;
We should love with a life-time's love in an hour,
  If the hours were few;
We should rest, not for dreams, but for fresher power
  To be and to do.

We should guide our wayward or wearied wills
  By the clearest light;
We should keep our eyes on the heavenly hills,
  If they lay in sight;
We should trample the pride and the discontent
  Beneath our feet;
We should take whatever a good God sent,
  With a trust complete.

We should waste no moments in weak regret,
 If the day were but one ;
If what we remember and what we forget
 Went out with the sun ;
We should be from our clamorous selves set free,
 To work or to pray,
And to be what the Father would have us be,
 If we had but a day.

IV.

"GATHER UP THE FRAGMENTS."

JOHN VI. 12.

DEAR Shepherd, who of old the listeners led
    Among the Galilean hills afar,
Who, when the even was come, the fainting fed,
While all the west with sunset hues flushed red,
    Grew dark, then brightened 'neath the evening star;
My soul, a listener through the fading light,
Yet hears thy voice, borne to me from the height.

The voice they heard, who, hasting, homeward pressed,
    Thoughtless, perhaps, though strengthened by thy
      hand,
Of greater feasts where they had been thy guests,
Of living bread thy lips for them had blessed,
    Of truths we all are slow to understand,
Till, fainting and athirst, and bowed with pain,
We turn to seek the Master's face again.

"Gather the fragments up!" O soul of mine,
　It matters not that in no Judean land
Thy ways were cast, yet have thy bread and wine
　Come ever surely from the Master's hand ;
　And even for thee were spoken this command,
To gather up—for him—the broken bread,
That from thy hand his hungry might be fed.

Troubled I hear, and, blending with thy tone,
　I catch the voices of the multitude,
Who struggle each with each, or faint alone,
　Or, cursing, cry for water and for food,
　Or question, " Who shall show us any good? "
The aged moan ; the child-hands are outspread
For the lost fragments of my daily bread.

Backward I look, beside youth's laughing stream,
　Over the meadows bathed by hope in light ;
Through the green pastures, brightened by love's dream,
　And to the valleys, wrapped in sorrow's night ;
　Or on the mountain summits cold and white,
Seeking for fragments of a broken life
For these, now fainting in the place of strife.

But, Lord, the stream of youth ran to the sea,
  And left no blossoms growing by its side;
And I have seen the hope-light fade and flee
  From the green pastures where my loves have died,
  And where my sorrows hide; but tears abide
And blood-marks trace the track o'er mountain sod
By which my tired soul sought to climb to God.

Yet, searching vainly for the things that bless,
  Some little drops of gratitude and prayer
Just keep my o'erturned cup from emptiness;
  Some memories of blessings strange and rare,
  Too sacred to be lost, too sad to share,
  Yet hold my heart back from a dull despair;
And I can always find, for Christ's dear shrine,
'Fragments from other lives dropped into mine.

'Tis not enough, O Lord! I still would seek
  The remnants of the strength in struggle lost,
The ruined fragments of the purpose weak,
  The wrecks of hope and love by shadows crossed,
  The shattered faith upon life's billows tossed;

And these, though emblems of my life's defeat,
I fain would bring, O Shepherd, to thy feet!

O Hand, that never breaks the bruised reed !
  O Voice, that held the waves in its control !
Speak peace, and let the fettered life be freed ;
  Pass grandly o'er the tossings of my soul ;
  Bind up my fragments to a perfect whole.
So, going forth, great in thy tenderness,
I may grow strong to cheer, and help, and bless.

V.

TO A FRIEND "ON THE NILE."

HOW, in the silence strange and sweet
That falls on the Egyptian night,
The voices of the years repeat
Tales of this monarch river's might,
Whose great heart, throbbing at our feet,
Goes on with ceaseless swell and beat ;

Goes on and on, while countless hearts
Of countless nations all are stilled ;
While countless years, that bore their part
In ages that were glory-filled,
Grew and declined beneath its smile,
And sleep in dust along the Nile.

O friend upon the Nile with me,
   Watching the tossings of the palms,
Tell me if e'er our days can be
   Fuller of blessings and of calms,
   Our music nearer like the psalms?

Tell me if 'neath the heavenly palms,
   Beside a river " crystal clear,"
We shall not know e'en deeper calms
   And softer psalms than we do here,
And, drifting 'neath God's smile the while.
Be happier there than on the Nile?

VI.

FORGIVEN.

ISAIAH XLIII. 25.

NOT on my forehead to lighten
    The fiery finger of pain ;
Not for a moment to slighten
    The bonds of my many-linked chain ;
Not to be freed from the scourging,
    Though faint when the smitings begin ;
But save me, dear Lord, from the surging
    Of the terrible sea of my sin.

Its mad waters drown my lamenting,
    Its black billows mockingly roll
In scorn of my fruitless repenting,
    In scorn at the fear of my soul.

It seemed such a calm sea of pleasure ;
　　Its voice was as soft as a song,
Till I trusted my life and my treasure,
　　And found it remorseless and strong.

I sink in a grief unavailing,
　　I reach through the dark for thy hand,
It guides—while my last strength is failing—
　　To a Rock in the treacherous sand ;
All the waters go over me, leaving
　　Me ruined and wrecked at *thy* feet :
Let me lie there and die there, believing
　　Forgiveness divine and complete.

Ah, me ! am I drowning and dreaming,
　　Like the stricken who die while they dream
Of a past and a future, both beaming
　　With fever's delirious gleam ?
Nay, nay ; it is real, I am going,
　　Unharmed by my pitiful loss,
Where the past and the future are glowing
　　Alike in the light of the cross.

2

And my soul is singing a pæan
   Louder than chant of the sea,
For the King of the waves Galilean
   Has stilled wilder waters for me ;
And the blackness is changing to brightness,
   While red waves of pardon o'erflow ;
My crimson is wool in its whiteness,
   My scarlet is purer than snow.

VII.

PRAISE.

HOW can I praise thee rightly, who have been
    So slow of heart, so dull to learn thy ways?
My soul is ready with its glad Amen
When others sing, and tries their songs again ;
    But all my singing does not sound like praise.

I thought, dear Lord, that e'en my muffled heart
    Might from its stifling silence break forth free,
And 'mong thy cheerful singers find a part,
    And add its might to all earth's minstrelsy ;
    But 'tis not thus I find it serveth thee.

Nay, I must e'en be still, my life at flood
    May overflow, but not in speech or song.
One may give love—as Jesus gave his blood,
    Each drop a power to lift the world from wrong ;
    And praise is sweet, but love and work are strong.

VIII.

WHY?

NOT because my palsied hand has gathered
　　Strength to take the idle weapons up;
Not because my lips have found the sweetness
　　Mingled with the bitter of my cup;

Not because the way in which I faltered
　　Has grown smoother, or my burden less;
Or because I see, thro' Fate's dark masking,
　　Where my smiters have been meant to bless;

Not because I see, in smoldering ashes,
　　Fires of hope and faith once more alight;
Or because my waiting has been resting,
　　Do I rise and ·gird me for the fight.

Gird me, though from wounds still faint and bleeding;
　　Walk erect, though weak, athirst, and faint;
And press onward to the end, unheeding
　　If my road be cheered by wayside saint.

'Tis enough that, lying in the shadows,
 Far away from saintly shrine or cross,
I have heard a voice of human music,
 Seen a smile that shamed defeat and loss;

Caught a glance from an illumined spirit,
 Throwing out, where life's high billows roll,
Light-house gleams of peace, which they inherit
 Who are strong in an unvanquished soul.

And because I see that sweet light falling
 Over wilder seas than I have tried,
Warning other barks in deeps appalling,
 Shining on to cheer, to help, to guide;

And because *I* saw it when *I* drifted,
 Wrecked and broken, on the shifting sand,
Have I lighted my small lamp, and lifted
 Up my life once more in trembling hand.

It may be the gleam of *my* small taper
 Shall o'ershine some rough or shadowed way;
So I clasp my weapons, take my burdens,
 And press forward to the eternal day.

IX.

A PICTURE.

ENTERED INTO REST, SEPT. 18, 1876, REV. BISHOP E. S. JANES.

ONLY a picture of an aged face,
    Wrinkled and seamed by years of thought and
      care;
Wearing serene its crown of silver hair,
Above a rugged brow that bears the trace
    Of earnest thoughts and softening touch of prayer.

As falls the mist upon the mountain side,
    Hiding the harsher tints of light and shade,
    Which showed where storm and wintry tempest
      played,
So falls the vail of chastened thought, to hide
    The rougher lines by life's stern conflicts made.

And have we only this? the pictured smile,
  The calm eyes that have wept their latest tears,
  And lost the earnest fire of early years,
Gaining this patient look of peace the while?
  A look that silences our murmuring fears.

Oh, no; these are not all! there was too much
  Of loving kindness toward his fellow-men,
  Of thoughtful care for every brother's pain,
Of *noble* things the Spoiler cannot touch,
  Or hearts forget, or even the *grave* retain.

And *deathless* are each kindly word or deed,
  The earnest purpose and the upright life,
The prayerful sowing of the precious seed,
The faithful word that bade the *right* God-speed,
  The helping hand held out in Freedom's strife.

So, though the kindly voice and step are still,
  And though we miss the smile his calm face wore,
  And grieve because we see him here no more,
We know life is not over, that he will
  Work for the Master—even as before.

That he will work—and wait—till those who grieve,
   Though their steps falter, and their eyes grow
      dim,
Shall, soon or late, his own deep peace receive,
And, one by one, their heavy burdens leave,
   And climb the shining way that leads to him.

X.

A PICTURE.

ENTERED INTO REST, AUGUST 13, 1876, CHARLOTTE, WIFE OF BISHOP JANES.

JUST as sweetly as fades the light
　　After the sun is gone,
Just as gently as through the night
　　The steady stars shine on,
Just as softly as Spring leaves come,
　　Or snow-flakes whiten the sod,
Passed she out from an earthly home
　　Into the home of God.

Never the rays of moon or sun
　　Fell on her face that day,
And only a heavenly artist's hand,
　　Could have left such light on clay.

2*

We knew that angel hands had wrought,
    Each day, at the soul within, ˉ
With loving touches of prayer and thought
    Hiding each trace of sin;

Sweeping the heavy shade of pain
    Over the smile of her face ;
And leaving the gleam of a Father's love,
    And the light of the cross in its place.
And so it was—their sweet work done,
    When the Master bade them cease,
There was left for our eyes to gaze upon,
    This beautiful picture of peace.

XI.

DEAD.

I BURIED a sorrow out of sight;
  It is dead! I said; it is dead!
I shrouded it well in mantle of white;
I made it a grave when the stars shone bright;   `
I pressed the sod till it covered it quite,
  And said, It is verily dead!
  It is dead! I said; it is dead!

I answered the asking of friendly eyes;
  It is dead! I said; it is dead!
I calmed my weeping; I chained my sighs;
My days ran laughter and low replies;
I gave back smiling for dumb surprise,
  And said, It is verily dead!
  It is dead! I said: it is dead!

I said it so often the wild waves heard ;
    It is dead ! they said ; it is dead !
The murmuring pines in the south wind stirred ;
The rush of waters, the song of bird,
All echoed together the same low word,
    It is dead ! they said ; it is dead !
    It is dead ! it is verily dead !

No growing grasses the grave revealed ;
    The sorrow is dead ! I said.
No deep scar showed where a hurt had healed ;
But a record was written, a book was sealed,
And a work was wrought in the world's wide field,
    While ever and ever I said,
    It is dead ! it is verily dead !

Ah, well for the world and the world's works' sake !
    It is dead ! I said ; it is dead !
But oh, for my heart ! if it once could wake,
Its pitiful bondage of silence break,
And find a voice for its dull, dumb ache !
    Nay, nay ; it is dead ! I said ;
    It is dead ! it is verily dead !

XII.

"IF THY RIGHT HAND OFFEND THEE."

NAY, *not* my right hand?
  It is scarred with its toil ; it hath never known
    rest ;
In the struggle of life it hath wrought with the best ;
It hath smitten the foes that assaulted my breast ;
It hath fought in my battles, fulfilled my command—
    Thou wilt spare my right hand?"

  "Nay, nay ; not so fast !
It *is* strong—it *hath* striven ; but aye for the right?
Can it hold its scars proudly to-day in my sight?
Hath it guarded thy bosom from darkness or light?
At my feet even now have its weapons been cast?
    Can I trust it at last?"

"Ah ! it quails at thy word ;
It hath scattered such seed as were better unsown ;
It hath garnered in fields that were never its own ;
It hath left its own garden with weeds overgrown ;
Yet it trembles and fears at the gleam of the sword.
　　Thou wilt pity it, Lord ? "

" And did I not heed
Thy pleading, and strengthen and cleanse and prepare
For work in my vineyard, my harvests to share?
Behold what rebellion hath answered my care !
Thy garners are empty, thou'rt crippled indeed ;
　　And yet dost thou plead ? "

" Nay, Lord, I am still !
See ! the hand is in thine ! If thou lovest me so,
There is mercy in smiting that lays me so low,
There are pardon and healing to follow the blow ;
Whole or maimed, weak or strong, if only thy will
　　Be wrought, I am still ! "

XIII.

TOIL AND REST.

FROM my window I can see the reapers
Bringing home their sheaves at set of sun ;
Drowsy bees are humming 'mid the creepers,
Over sweetness gained and labor done.

Peasant women from the field are bringing
Little rosy children, tired of play,
Who, within the sound of mother's singing,
Slept or sported in the grass all day.

" Blest the toil that sweetens rest and pleasure,"
Sighs the evening wind through closing flowers ;
"Blest each humble hand that wrested treasure
From the golden storehouse of the hours."

Throbs the earth with pulse of strong endeavor ;
I alone, behind my prison bars,
Hold my hands up empty, and can never
Welcome the calm coming of the stars.

I am weary, too ; yet restful even
  On no harvest-work of mine has smiled ;
And no song of mine has sweetness given
  Even to the slumbers of a child.

I have lost the Hand the whole world guiding
  To the fields where humble souls rejoice,
And earth's harmonies are changed to chiding.
  Wind and leaf and wave, with one low voice,

Sadly talk of life that yields no sweetness,
  Waking mournful echo in my breast,
Till I, quickened, yearn for the completeness
  Of a toil that earns the evening's rest ;

Till I hasten to my own late sowing,
  In the fields forever stretching wide,
Where, of old, one at the last hour going,
  Found his penny at the eventide.

Homburg, Germany, July 18th.

XIV.

TWO AND ONE.

TWO mountain streamlets seeking
 Lone ways to the same sea ;
Two tones that need but echoes
 To make them harmony ;
Two clouds at sunset ranging
 The western fields of light,
One glowing gold, one changing
 Its purple into white ;
Two pilgrims walking lonely,
 Rough ways to the same shrine ;
Two right hands lifted upward
 For cups of life's red wine.

Two small streams make together
 A river swift and strong ;
Two voices make new music,
 If blended in one song ;

And in the western heaven
　　Strange, wondrous tints unfold,
When cloud in white and purple
　　Meets cloud in crimson and gold ;
And a smoother road leads upward
　　Than lonely saint e'er knew,
Through fragrant lands, where one strong hand
　　Must gather the grapes for two.

So music is wedded to music,
　　And stream and stream are one,
And cloud is the bride of cloudlet
　　In the palace of the sun ;
And a life that is weak and wanting
　　Rounds to a perfect whole,
When spirit is one with spirit,
　　And soul is wedded to soul.

XV.

AMONG THE SAINTS.

ON THE CATHEDRAL AT MILAN.

THERE'S a winding stairway in the tower,
  Leading upward ever high and higher,
From the silence of the old cathedral ;
From the shadow of the ancient columns,
Standing strong in still and solemn grayness,
'Neath the fretted roof's uplifted arches ;
From the windows, where the common sunlight,
Through the glowing robes of saints transmitted,
Grows a golden glory, flecked with rubies ;
From the crypt, where silver lamps' faint flicker
On the crystal coffins and the jewels
Makes them smile with cold, unmeaning glitter,
Mocking ghastly dust they cannot cover ;
From the lifted cross and gorgeous altar ;

From the hurried priest's monotonous droning,
And the echo of the faint responses ;
From the kneelers, idling at their praying,
Swiftly slipping beads through careless fingers ;
From the footfall of the curious strangers,
And the truer pleading of the beggars—
Halt and maimed, for whom is no Bethesda ;
Leprous limbed, for whom there flows no Jordan ;
Blind, who, waiting ever by the wayside,
Never hear the step of heavenly Healer ;
From the organ's grand, majestic hymning,
And the bell that, in its mighty sweetness,
Gives the soul of the cathedral utterance,
Like a great heart's high, tumultuous throbbing,
Finding echo in the hidden places.
—Mounting slow this stairway in the tower,
All the mingled sounds are lost in silence.
Lost the dimness, gold and ruby tinted,
In a canopy of white and turquoise,
God's o'ershadowing clouds and arch of azure.
Now the giant temple is below us ;
Far below us the majestic city;

Quivering like a restless human creature,
Pulsing with the pain of human heart-aches;
So alive with hopes of myriad mortals,
With the floods of love, of death, of passion
Finding veins in every street and by-way—
Veins that leave their dead at this wide portal
When the floods are gone and tides are ebbing.

This great temple seems almost immortal,
Even as if the dead hands that upreared it,
With unseen and ever silent touches,
Swept away the dust of its decaying ;
Till it stands so sacred in its whiteness,
So unsullied in its marble vesture,
That, methinks, Jerusalem the Golden,
Coming down from God with fair adorning,
If it had but need of one fair temple
For the kings to bring their glory into,
Then, methinks, the Bride let down from
    heaven,
With the glory of the Lord upon her,
Of her golden streets and walls of jasper,

Of her pearly gates swung wide forever,
Of her light, beyond the sun's clear shining,
Would not find this house of God unworthy.

Here have human faith, and love, and longing
Crystallized in forms of grace and beauty,
Till each slender shaft, and shrine, and column
Is a tear, or prayer, or hope, embodied ;
Voices something that were else unspoken.
Every statue of the white three thousand,
Waiting, silent, through the drifting ages,
While the Italian sod takes to her bosom,
One by one, the countless generations
Who have lifted up their eyes in dying
To the marble faces shining on them,
Has its voice of blessing or of comfort.
Glorious company of saints and martyrs,
In their hands the palms of triumph bearing,
On their brows the peace of those who conquered.
Calm, sweet souls, who are to-day's possession,
Whose good deeds, to every clime belonging,
Bridge, with blessing and with inspiration,

All the seas of years that swell between us.
No more seem they marble statues only,
Keeping guard above the old cathedral ;
But each niche reveals a face transfigured
With the peace of Him "who overcometh."
All the patient look of calm endurance,
All the upraised, tearful glance of longing,
Over-swept by some high hope of service
To be wrought for those who still must struggle.
These are dwellers in the higher temple ;
Human hearts have shrined their life and story,
Human lives have seen their hidden glory,
By their helping grown to greater meetness
For that chiefest joy, the sure indwelling
Of the love that makes our life's completeness.

Far below us lies the living city ;
Calm before us spreads the wide Campagna ;
All the hillsides smile with countless vineyards ;
All the slopes show silvery shine of olives ;
And, beyond, rise up the glorious mountains,
The eternal mountains of the Alpland.

Far to southward sleeps the land of blossoms,
Dreams the Italy, that more than ever
Should arise and don her beauteous garments ;
Should lift up her voice in purer praising,
That no longer down her mountain passes
Or 'cross seas, her foes shall come upon her ;
That the dust is swept from off her altars ;
That the iron chains of superstition
Bind no more the spirits of her people ;
That her worshiping may yet be worthy
Of her temples and the God above them.

XVI.

ENDURANCE.

FOR deeps of human suffering or joy no measure
    Into our hands is given ;
We cannot know our brother's loss or treasure,
    His anguish or his heaven.

Ofttimes the arrowy sharpness of a sorrow,
    Piercing life's common calm,
Smites hidden rocks of comfort, which to-morrow
    O'erflow with healing balm.

Ofttimes we calmest find grief's turbid river
    Who trembled on its brink ;
And oft the cup at which our blanched lips quiver
    Holds wine of hope to drink.

3

'Neath burdens that we staggered in the taking
We walk erect at length ;
And bitter blows that bow us e'en to breaking
Reveal our secret strength.

XVII.

THE PRODIGAL'S RETURN.

I.

BACK to thy feet, O my Father !
  Wearied and stricken and sore,
Dragging a heavier burden
  Than ever a prodigal bore ;
Coming with worn feet that falter,
  Hands that are crimsoned with stain,
And a heart that can lay on thine altar
  Only its sin and its pain.

II.

I changed the white robes of thy favor
  For garments tattered and soiled ;
The fields where thou badest me labor
  The weeds and the foxes have spoiled.

I turned from the fruits of thy vineyard,
   To feed on the husks with the swine,
And left the pure springs of thy mercy
   For cups of the rioter's wine.

III.

And now to thy feet I am coming,
   Saddened, ashamed, and defiled,
And I ask for the bread of a servant—
   Not worthy the name of a child.
I wait, in the dust, for thy greeting ;
   If it come with the stroke of thy rod,
Spare it not, if it hasten the meeting
   Of a penitent heart and its God.

IV.

O stained hands ! cleansed by thy grasping !
   O bleeding feet ! healed in thy ways !
Leave thy sins, and press onward, close-clasp-
     ing
   The cross of my shame and thy praise.

Till the tearful eyes, healed of their blindness,
Shall see, from the lowliest place,
The wonderful mercy and kindness
That shines in thy pardoning face.

XVIII.

MARY BEARING THE DOVES TO SACRIFICE.

A PICTURE ON THE WALL.

M Y lifted eyes behold a fair child's face,
   Under a vail of woman's holiest thought,
O'ershadowed by the mystery of grace
   And mystery of mercy God hath wrought.

Down through the dim old Temple moving slow,
   Her drooping lids scarce lifted from the ground,
As if she dimly heard the distant flow
   Of far-off seas of grief she could not sound.

I think the angels scarce could count it sin,
   If, underneath the vail that hid her eyes,
They, seeing all things, saw the soul within
   Knew more of mother-love than sacrifice.

She walks erect, like one all undefiled ;
   Back from her throat the loose robe falls apart,
And, e'en as she would clasp her royal child,
   She holds the dovelets to her mother-heart.

No white wing trembles 'neath her pitying palm ;
   No feather flutters in this last warm nest ;
And so she bears them on, while solemn psalm
   Drowns the prophetic whisper in her breast.

Sweet Hebrew Mother ! many a woman shares
   Thy crucifixion of her hopes and loves ;
And in her arms to death unshrinking bears
   Her precious things, as thou thy turtle-doves.

But often, ere upon the marble floor
   Has died the echo of the parting feet,
Our gifts prove worthless ; thine is evermore,
   The gift of gifts, transcendent and complete.

We have our little treasures, each our own,
  And, one by one, we see them sacrificed.
Thou, "blessed among women!" thou, alone,
  Couldst give to God—from thine own arms—
    the Christ.

XIX.

ALONE.

A FRAID to dwell alone, O coward heart !
When he, whose hand hath set thee thus apart,
Built up thy hedges, closed thine open gate,
Knows what it is to stand outside, and wait ?

Oh ! think how oft—his locks with night dews wet—
He trod the shadowy gloom of Olivet ;
How vainly sought one loving soul, to share
Gethsemane's sad hour of midnight prayer.

How human hearts gave back, for love, their hate ;
Till, smitten, scorned, and mocked, and desolate,
His aching heart broke with this dying moan :
" My God ! my God ! why am I left alone ? "

Before his cross, O tired soul ! be still ;
Accept the path he shows thee ; let his will

3*

Be guide and comfort ; so, however drear
The way may seem to thee, he will be near !

Hearing his voice, what other canst thou need ?
Seeing his smile, thy days are fair indeed.
Divinest fellowship may be thine own—
Say, soul, art still afraid to be alone ?

XX.

LIGHT IN DARKNESS.

THE fire burns low, the shadows gleam and fade,
　　And darkness lingers where the sunset played ;
A hand of silence on my lips is laid—
　　　I cannot find the light !

One eager longing fills my clouded breast ;
I wait the coming of a heavenly guest :
Thou, who of old in Bethany didst rest,
　　　Tarry with me to-night !

With goodly fare my table is not spread ;
Hot tears have mingled with my wine and bread ;
I cannot pour upon thy blessed head
　　　The spikenard rare and sweet.

But if my few poor gifts thou condescend
To take, thy taking worthiness will lend,
And I will pour my soul out, O my Friend !
　　　Like Mary, at thy feet !

My soul, consumed by sin's corroding rust ;
My soul, that spurned the stars and loved the dust ;
My soul, that longs at last for love and trust,
  Is all I have to bring.

I strain my gaze now for one gleaming star,
I sit in darkness with my door ajar,
That I may hear thy footsteps from afar,
  The footsteps of my King !

And I *do* hear, though clouds thy visage hide ;
I reach my hand out thro' the shadowy tide
Of doubts and fears, and on the other side
  Lo, it is clasped in thine !

I shuddering feel the nail-prints in the palm ;
But oh ! the wound drops healing, and a balm
Of tenderness, that blesses with a calm
  Of peace and love divine.

XXI.

A PRAYER.

WEARIED and tired and worn,
  Loathing what is, dreading what is to be,
Shrinking from burdens that must still be borne,
    Father, I come to thee!

I lay my burdens down
  One moment, that my hands thy cross may take.
When shall I lift them up to take the crown
    Given for Christ's dear sake?

I'm wearied with the heat,
  And still the sands grow hotter 'neath my tread;
Beside no cool streams walk my aching feet,
    No shade is o'er my head.

I come to thee for rest,
  Bringing thee love and trust—both weak thro'
    pain ;
Oh ! lift me till I lie upon thy breast,
    Love me to peace again.

And lay thy precious hand,
  In softest touches, on my head to-day,
And let me by thine own strong breath be fanned
    Through all the desert way.

Then, though my heart be sad,
  Though I am weary, and the way seem long,
Thy blessed presence here shall make me glad,
    In thee I shall be strong.

XXII.

- ## VENETIA LIETH DEAD.

O PURPLE Adriatic ! that wore upon thy breast
   The splendor of the Orient, the glory of the
      West !
O rare and royal wooer ! O sea ! whose throbbing
      tide
Enfolded fair Venetia, and won her for thy bride ;
Till, robed in beauteous garments, with white, un-
      sandaled feet,
She walked upon the waters, her lord, her king to
      meet.
Soft, soft the vow and sweet the kiss with which
      the maiden wed,
But softer let the farewell be.   Venetia lieth dead !

Thy waters, Adriatic, still kiss her icy feet ;
The winds still bear thy love-song in music low and
      sweet ;

Still kindly bend above her the glowing eastern skies ;
But the tender golden glory reflected in her eyes,
The rainbow hues of promise, the purple of her
    pride,
Have faded to the dimness that marked the eventide.
The rose tint of her gladness, through all the warm
    air shed,
Has paled to moonlight whiteness. Venetia lieth dead!

Where sped the bright-winged gondola along the
    tideless street,
Whose paths could never echo the tread of human feet,
Still all day long the boatmen ply upon their silent
    track ;
But the gorgeous bird of paradise is changed to
    raven black ;
And where the songs of merriment fell on the air
    of yore,
The boatman's muttered curse beats time to music
    of the oar ;
The fluttering silken canopy above the dreamer's head
Is changed to pall-like drapery. Venetia lieth dead !

Her shining marble palaces show dim, time-black-
ened walls ;

The shadowy ghosts of grander days haunt her de-
serted halls ;

The doves that came from eastern lands to nestle
in her breast

Have felt a chill beneath their wings, and sought a
warmer nest ;

Her Winged Lion croucheth low beneath the Austrian's hand ;

Her banner traileth in the dust, that brightened sea
and land ;

Her faith and hope in sackcloth, with ashes on her
head,

And dust upon her altars. Venetia lieth dead !

So, shorn of all her beauty, and robbed of all her
might,

Fold thy soft waves about her and shroud her out
of sight.

Too long she walked in freedom to bear the captive's
pain,   [chain.

Her white hands held a scepter too long to wear a

So, when from out her heaven dropped the star of
  Liberty,
Queen of the Adriatic, Bride of the Southern Sea,
What marvel that she languished, that, on her bil-
  lowy bed,
Unheeding all thy moaning, Venetia lieth dead?

O silent city ! sleeping beneath Italia's sun,
With thy last thoughts of freedom departing one by
  one,
Like specters that, unrecognized, from out the past
  arise,
And glide in swift procession over thy Bridge of
  Sighs ;
Over the weary Bridge of Sighs, that erst its burden
  bore
From the stately palace portal e'en to the prison
  door ;
The prison door, behind whose bars, with the waters
  for her bed,
And Italia's sky above her, Venetia lieth dead !

VENICE, 1865.

XXIII.

VENETIA WAKES AGAIN.

NOT in her early beauty, not in her robes of
pride,
As when the orange blossoms crowned the sea's transcendent bride ;
But clad in every color Italia's flag unfurls,
She puts aside her sackcloth, and gathers up her
pearls,
And binds them on her brow once more, and counts
them as the tears
From eyes that watched for freedom through all the
weary years ;
And casting from her fettered limbs the Austrian's
galling chain,
She lifts her face up to the sun.   " Venetia wakes
again ! "

Again upon each crowded bridge waits an exultant
    throng,
Again on every silent street rings out the boatman's
    song,
And pennons float from mast and tower and marble
    balcony,
And cheers and waving banners greet the army of
    the free.
Not with the tramp of hurrying feet or mail-clad
    warriors' tread,
Not with the captives at their heels or conquerors at
    their head,
Not with the canopy of gold above the glittering train,
Or gorgeous pageantry of old "Venetia wakes again !"

But radiant with the dawning of future life and
    strength,
The dawning of the perfect day she shall behold at
    length ;
And happy hands shower flowers down, laden with
    tears and prayers,
On every gondola that slow the proud procession bears.

The angels of deliverance are welcomed none the less
That 'stead of royal robes they wear the Garibaldian dress,
And bear within their strong right hands a sword that knows no stain,
A scepter, at whose lightest touch "Venetia wakes again."

O woe to thee, Italia ! if, sheltered in thy breast,
She finds not there her truest *life*, as well as truest rest.
And woe to thee ! if bearing now thy flag, thy shield, thy name,
Thou lift her not from darkness, and redeem her not from shame.
Free from the mountains to the sea, thy children gathered home,
One prouder day yet waits for thee, when thy banner floats o'er Rome.
But when thy song of triumph gains that *last* exultant strain,
Still let it keep this glad refrain, "Venetia wakes again ! "

VENICE, 1866.

XXIV.

TRUE FREEDOM.

"For Freedom is not secured by full enjoyment of what is desired, but by controlling the desire."—*Epictetus.*

STRANGELY on our hurried human living,
    On our restless strife and eager scheming,
On our stubborn habit of resistance
To whatever mocks or thwarts our wishes,
Falls the wisdom of the old-time teacher.

Strange—yet, when our deepest souls make answer,
They but give an echo to the lessons ;
And we know, by subtle inward teaching,
Truths the outward sense denies or questions.
Thus we know that he alone hath riches
Who hath proved the greatness of a little ;
He alone hath store of heavenly treasure
Whom God loveth as a cheerful giver ;

That he only walks in truest freedom
Who can bear his chains without a murmur ;
And that he is victor over trouble
Who hath learned the blessedness of yielding,
And possesseth his own soul in patience.

So it is ; we may be ''more than conquerors ;''
'' More than conquerors'' through One who
   loved us ;
One whose strength is in our weakness perfect ;
One who meets our emptiness with fullness ;
One who said, '' Who saveth life shall lose it ;
He who giveth findeth life eternal.''

\

XXV.

THE LAST OF THE SUMMER.

I SEE them again, my own hill-lands,
  The mountains I used to know
When my shadows were falling westward,
  And my days were all aglow
  With the sun of long ago.

I have no need to remember
  The picture of each old place,
For the touch of the young September
  On Nature's familiar face
  Has given the old-time grace;

The grace of the day when the sunshine
  Creeps softly and slow toward the west;
The faint, nameless shade, scarce a shadow,
  That holds a dim promise of rest,
  Which marks its own hour as the best.

A grace which the dying summer
  Threw, like a mantle, down
On mountain, and field, and woodland,
  Where, living, she wore her crown—
  The crown in the dust laid down.

It hangs o'er the hillside forests
  In many a misty fold,
And the life is gone from their greenness,
  And the mountains look blighted and cold,
  Like strong men suddenly old.

The tender green of the grasses
  Is changed to a lifeless gray ;
I have seen the velvet cushions
  In places where penitents pray,
  That looked like the fields to-day.

And the whole earth seems a temple,
  Where, notes of praise between,
An undertone of sorrow
  Echoes in aisles of green,
  For a dead and discrowned queen.

4

And the gay and glorious autumn
  Reluctant comes to reign,
As if she shrank from startling
  With light and joy again
  This vague, unspoken pain.

But a crimson banner, flying
  From one lone maple tree,
Gives to the wind a promise
  Of glory that will be,
  When the summer shade shall flee.

The woods may burn with color,
  And the sun the hill-tops kiss;
From all their royal robing
  My heart a charm shall miss,
  And no day be like this.

I shall open mine eyes to the glory,
  I shall join the harvest praise;
But I cannot carry over
  Into the gayer ways
  What died in the summer days.

XXVI.

(THE LORD IS MY SHEPHERD.

23D PSALM, FOR A CHILD.

THE Lord is my Shepherd," and I am his
lamb,
One of the smallest and weakest I am ;
Yet by his bounty daily I'm fed,
In his green pastures tenderly led.

Kind is my Shepherd, and large is his fold,
Daily he welcomes the young as the old ;
Tenderly watching, in waking and sleep,
Over us evermore guard doth he keep.

Sometimes the way where he leadeth his sheep
Groweth for child-feet dark and too steep ;
Then doth he lift me close to his breast,
Bearing me upward to places of rest.

He hath green pastures lying afar,
Needing no sunlight, needing no star ;
There from his presence the lambs never stray,
Thither he leadeth me nearer each day.

I hear of a valley and shadow of death ;
I see but green meadows illumined by faith ;
Whatever the journey still trustful I am,
For the Lord is my Shepherd, and I am his lamb.

XXVII.

THE EVERY-DAY SORROW.

THE troubled tide of tangible despairing
  Beats never unconsoled ;
Not so the long, low swell of anguish, bearing
  Dumb sorrows manifold.

The common griefs of common souls, whose level
  Is mortals' low estate ;
Whose voices, deadened by some loud woe's revel,
  In sobbing silence wait ;

Wait for one answering cry of recognition,
  One star athwart their sky,
One promise of a far-off, fair fruition
  For hopes that waiting die ;

And, dying, walk again in ghostly starkness,
    Peopling the gloomy gray
That makes their heaven murkier than darkness,
    And farther from the day.

For these where is the light?   Shall that bright portal
    Which, soon or late, swings wide
For every soul, reveal a joy immortal
    Secure the other side?

Shall some their crosses lift, till night upon them
    Transfigures all below,
And wear our crowns so long ere they have won them
    That all their glory know—

And these, who, bending, drag a cross in sadness,
    Their faces to the dust,
Not carry palms at last? or know the gladness
    Of souls that rest and trust?

Is it slow-slipping beads, or patient folding
    Of stainéd hands in prayer,

That makes them purer ? or the faithful holding
    Of what God gives to bear ?

Not all the gathered wisdom of the sages
    Can guess God's hidden ways,
And yet the slow unfolding of the ages
    Must still show forth his praise.

And all this mystery of pain, our spirits
    Can neither bear nor break,
May not be mystery to souls who bear it
    In love and for love's sake.

XXVIII.

"A LAMP TO THY FEET, AND A LIGHT TO THY PATH."

A LAMP to thy feet—not a splendor
    Lighting the hills afar ;
Not a radiance, solemn and tender,
    Of moonlight or glimmering star.
All around may be shrouded in shadow
    And dimness and mist of the night ;
But be it o'er mountain or meadow,
    Before us the path shall be light !

Not light with the glow of the morning,
    Flooded with sunshine sweet ;
Not e'en the faint gleam of the dawning,
    But only a "lamp to the feet."

If all the long road stretched in whiteness,
   And wide fields smiled in the day,
Should we move swiftly on in the brightness,
   Or linger and dream by the way?

He knoweth, who, guiding the stranger
   Safely in darkness and light,
Hath hidden the glory and danger
   Alike from our wandering sight.
He knoweth, who, walking before us
   Bearing the glimmering lamp,
How somber the shade that hangs o'er us,
   How we shiver and shrink in the damp.

For *His* locks are wet with the night-dews,
   His feet are bleeding and torn,
As, wearying under *our* burden,
   He treads in *our* pathway the thorn.
Though His lamp lights one step and one only,
   There's the mark of *His* foot in the sod ;
And the way may be stormy or lonely,
   It ends in the smile of our God !

4*

XXIX.

NOTHING LOST.

THERE is no heart, however lost and straying
　　From the green pastures and the narrow road,
But sees afar, sometimes, the soft light playing
　　Around the summit of the mount of God ;

And seeing, longs to try the upward climbing
　　Of that hard path that leads away from night,
To where the sin-dulled ear can catch the chiming
　　Of souls triumphant who have reached the height.

And sometimes hands well trained to evil uses
　　Will drop the weapons of their sin and strife,
And take instead the cross of one. who chooses
　　To lose all things and gain eternal life.

'Tis true, the eye that sees the mountain glowing
　May turn to shadows ere the day is done ;
The feet most eager in their upward going
　May falter ere the race is well begun ;

The hands may drop the burdens and the crosses;
　The quickened ear forget the heavenly song ;
The wrecked soul drift, forgetful of its losses,
　And all the right go back again to wrong.

And yet while life goes on—a restless fever,
　With good ennobled and with evil curst—
Each restless longing, and each grand endeavor,
　And each high hope are, to that fever's thirst,

Like one more drop from a celestial river
　That waters all the region, wide and fair,
Where wanderers go no more out forever,
　When once have shut the golden gates of prayer.

XXX.

THE KNEELING PLACE.

THRO' somber temples taper lights are gleaming.
Often God's light instead
Thou hast, through window small the white moon
streaming,
And stars o'erhead.
Up thro' the hushed air of these sacred places
White prayers are drifted.
Here rise the pleadings low of sad, still faces
In tears uplifted.
High thoughts, and words, and music strong and
sweet
May be Faith's token ;
But tears that fall in love at Jesus' feet
Are prayers unspoken.

XXXI.

"THE BELLS OF LYNN."

READ ON THE CAMPAGNA AT ROME.

"BELLS OF LYNN," BY HENRY W. LONGFELLOW.—*Atlantic Monthly.*

UNDER the calm sky bending over Rome
  I read a book from home.
Slowly its treasures open to the sun ;
  I grasp them, one by one,
And heeding not the wavering sunlight's play
  On tower and town that day,
Or how it brightens with its crimson glow
  The Alban hills of snow,
Or that the Tiber wanders at my feet
  With murmur low and sweet,
I see as in a dream the white sheep pass
  On the Campagna grass,
And hear the chirp of birds and voices young
  The olive trees among ;
The squalid beggars haunting each fair spot
  Pray, and I heed them not ;

The dark Priest kneeling by the wayside shrine
        Has thought nor prayer of mine;
The distant wastes of ruin only seem
        The fabrics of a dream;
For over all the stretch of billowy sea
        A voice has come to me,
So far, so dim, and yet so real and near,
        I bend my head to hear,
And thro' the Eternal City's swell of tone
        Breaks that one sound alone:
Above the noise without, the jar within,
        I hear the Bells of Lynn
Speak low to me as, in the olden time,
        I heard your dear notes chime;
And, as a tired child hears a mother's voice,
        I listen and rejoice.
I still am gathering pebbles all the day—
        It is no longer play—
And not forever by the sounding sea
        Can my poor gleanings be;
But 'mong the ruins and by thorny road
        Which nobler steps have trod,

Burdened and weary oft, I upward press
        Beyond all weariness ;
And breaking softly through the ways of pain,
        To hear thy voice again
Is earnest that the rest shall soon begin.
        Speak on, O Bells of Lynn !
Tell me if round the gray rocks of Nahant
        Still, still the wild winds chant ;
If ever, in your music's wandering low,
        It chanced where violets grow ;
If 'mong the mosses and upon the hill
        The wild rose climbeth still ;
If you go out to meet the ships at sea
        With winds for company ;
Bearing to wanderers the thoughts of home,
        As here to me in Rome.
Tell me if underneath the willow's shade
        Any new graves are made ;
If—but I catch the trembling of thy strain,
        And will not ask again.
It needs not voice of wind or wave or bell
        To tell me—all is well.

I know not how the golden day has sped ;
    The home book is unread ;
On dome and spire and mount and ruined wall
    Softly the shadows fall,
And far above the distant city's din
    I hear the Bells of Lynn.
The shepherd leads his white lambs to the fold,
    While round the ruin old
There clings the glory of the setting sun ;
    And slowly, one by one,
The penitents forsake the wayside shrine ;
    While the unchanging sign
Of Christ's dear love, uplifted in the light,
    Gleams still and white ;
And vesper music with its healing calm
    Falls on the air like balm.
Still I am seeing, even thro' my tears,
    The home of early years ;
And hearing, through the sound of pain or sin,
    Only the Bells of Lynn;
Thro' all that is, and all that might have been,
    The dear old Bells of Lynn.

XXXII.

A WISH.

I.

MY life has climbed to its topmost steep ;
  I see the slopes on the downward side ;
I have seen my sea at its fullest tide,
And watched the darkling waters creep,
Out to the deep, where a dreamless sleep
  Waits whatever has lived and died.

II.

And I backward throw one line of prayer,
  A frail thread over the ways I've trod,
  That the valley glooms, and the thorny sod,
And the desert's burning paths of care
Change to the gleam of pastures fair,
  Under your step as you climb to God.

XXXIII.

A PRAYER.

I LONG to take the wine of love and faith,
　Which, overflowing once in crimson flood,
Swept over all the wastes of sin and death,
　A great tide welling from the heart of God ;
Which flowed and ebbed, and to his feet swept
　　back
　A world's heart cleansed in blood.

Was it alone for one of old—beloved—
　Saviour, to lay his head upon *thy* breast ?
And wilt thou not to-day take to thy bosom
　A heart that only there can find its rest ?
And say again, "To whom is much forgiven
　Shall it be given to love and serve Me best"?

XXXIV.

THANKS FOR FLOWERS.

HOW shall I mold the blossoms of my speech
　　To forms as fair as those to-night you bring ?
How grasp the garland just beyond my reach,
　　Who always stammer when I need to sing?

If *I* had thoughts as bright as flowers are,
　　And words that made them gleam like drops of dew,
Words that held fragrance, life, and beauty rare,
　　Then I would make a wreath of them for you.

But, while outside the fields are fair enough,
　　And with your gift my room is all aglow,
In mine own garden, rocky-soiled and rough,
　　Things worthy of your taking will not grow.

The fairest buds with which it once was filled
  Clouds frowned upon oftener than sunshine smiled ;
Some drooped in spring, and some were winter-killed,
  And some grew old while I was but a child.

Here is one little sprig of mignonette ;
  It grew close 'neath the shelter of the wall ;
And here's one pansy by the night-dews wet,
  Too hardy to die early—that is all.

But, cheered and rested by your kindly thought,
  I'll throw my gardens open to the sun,
And maybe, some time, when my work is wrought,
  And I need flowers, I shall find more than one.

If it be true—that saying quaint and old—
  " Kind deeds are golden grain that cannot die,
But bringeth to the sower many fold,"
  Then *I shall* bring you blossoms by and by.

XXXV.

LABORARE EST ORARE.

THE fleecy clouds are climbing from the rivers,
 The distant mountain-tops are all aglow
With morning's early light, that, glancing, quivers
 Among the firs that crown the crags below.

Give back again my pilgrim staff, my Father,
 To guard my steps adown the dizzy height ;
For, long before the evening shadows gather,
 I journey toward a country out of sight.

O Father ! tempt me not. I well remember
 When, blind and baffled by the blasts of fate,
And chilled by years that were one long December,
 I staggered fainting to thy convent gate.

Can I forget thy ministry of healing,
  The cup of wine, the sleep in spotless cell,
The hand of benediction, the appealing
  Of cross and saint and shrine and vesper-bell,

The days of calm, the nights of solemn splendor,
  The heights of silence, where e'en murmurs cease,
The spirit's tender and serene surrender
  To the incoming of abiding peace?

Oh ! sweet indeed the rest upon the mountains,
  This strength from out the everlasting hills,
This draught of life from purest upland fountains,
  This sight of Heaven that all my vision fills.

But, Father, here I came through desert dangers ;
  I held my breaking staff with bleeding hand,
And left behind me weary, stricken strangers
  Athirst and fainting on the shifting sand.

The desert wells were dry ; my flask was broken ;
  Too frail for mine own weakness was my rod ;
The hot skies gave their lifted eyes no token ;
  No rain-cloud answered to their cry to God.

They pilgrims too, alas ! with none to love them ;
  Their spent lives languished, while God quickened
    mine ;
Rain fell for me—the heavens were brass above them ;
  I only reached the mountains, gained the shrine.

True, they were spared my long and dreary climbing,
  My battling with the tempest and the cold ;
But oh ! my Father, they have missed the chiming
  Of my sweet bells, my shepherd, and my fold.

E'en here, on these cool steeps, hot throbs of anguish
  Repeat in mine own veins their pulse of pain ;
I, too, beneath the desert-fever languish ;
  Their striving drowns my peace, their loss my
    gain.

Their hunger robs my daily bread of sweetness,
  Their moans thread sadly my triumphant psalm.
Let me go down to share in its completeness
  Their woes, or lift them up to share this calm.

Oh, idle rest, while dearer souls are straying !
Oh, selfish joy, while these are unforgiven !
Oh, vanity of vague and voiceless praying !
If but for this our stained souls were shriven.

Nay ; let me tarry on the heights no longer.
Round purer heart I wrap the pilgrim dress ;
In purer touch the trembling staff is stronger ;
My face is steadfast toward the wilderness,

To help the helpless, strengthen those who falter,
To lead to light the sorrowing and blind,
To reach once more my sacred mountain altar ;
But not to leave the weaker ones behind.

Should such sweet grace to my rude hands be given
To bind up wounds, to lift the stricken up ;
Each sufferer shall see the smile of Heaven
Outshining on him from the healing cup.

And should I perish by the way, another
Will surely struggle up to where I rest ;
By mantle, scrip, and staff will know a brother,
And, by this little cross upon my breast,

Will know my soul has dwelt in peace up higher,
  Will take my little store of oil and wine,
And quickened by the glow of inward fire,
  Mount e'en to heavenly heights beyond my shrine.

But see ! the mists are fleeing while I linger,
  The distant hills have lost their rosy glow,
And underneath the touch of Day's soft finger
  Have wrapped themselves in robes of purest snow.

I bend my head, my Father, for thy blessing ;
  I go—not like the mountains—clad in white ;
Yet falls on me, like mother's hand caressing,
  The silent benediction of the light.

XXXVI.

MY MOTHER'S BIRTHDAY.

JANUARY 18, 1874.

ON THE NILE.

SHE is lying there upon the hill-side,
     And her grave is covered by the snow-wreaths;
Snow-white blossoms hang on all the laurels,
And the willows bend beneath their burden,
And the dead leaves and the earth's brown bosom
Share with her the robe of radiant whiteness.
She is calm and pale and very silent,
And her hands are folded from their labor,
And she does not hear my worn heart call her,
"Mother, wake, and keep with me thy birthday!"

I am here beside the sullen river
Whose o'erflowing made the nations mighty,

With the desert mountains lifting round me,
And the wind-swept changing sands, revealing
Day by day grave shadows, dim and somber,
Kingly tombs that mark the desolation
Promised in the burning words of prophets.
Yet I lift mine eyes up to the palm-boughs,
Waving softly by the yellow Nile bank ;
And my soul flies swiftly from the Winter,
Swiftly from my own hot desert pathway,
To another land, where we, together—-
Mother of the blessed heart of patience,
Child of wayward will and wearied spirit—
Meet as truly as we met in birthdays
Ere to thee had come the bliss of dying,
Ere to me had come the grief to lose thee.

In that land where thou art now a dweller
Snows nor burning suns can bar our meeting,
And the flow of an eternal river,
And the breath of winds in banks of greenness,
Gives me from afar a voice of greeting.

There thou hast the palms without the desert;
There the plains on which no blight has rested;
There the mounts of God that hide no secrets,
As these hills that hide the tombs of monarchs
And the graves of nations long since buried;
There thou hast the bliss of the beloved.
Evermore I know the little children
Come around thee with their old caressing.
There the years slip by, and birthdays find thee
With the pain-marks faded from thy forehead;
With the eyes that watched us in our childhood
Only growing deeper, sweeter, clearer
With the mother-love, that brings thee nearer
All that's holy, while it holds *us* dearer,
Caring even when our weak hearts wander.

Mother, when this day was at its dawning,
Crept I softly in the early twilight
To thy heart, and left there all my burden;
And I felt the angels, who must love thee,
Could not bring a gift THY heart would prize more
Than the love that climbs e'en to thy heaven

From the spot, where, in her upward journey,
Thine own child has lain down worn and tired.

Sweet to thee must be celestial hymning;
But I know, through all the heavenly praises,
Thou hast bent thine ear to catch *my* whispers ;
Thou hast reached thy soft hand down to bless me ;
Thou art happier in thy life of gladness
For the mighty love thy child doth bring thee.

XXXVII.

A MOTHER'S QUESTION.

I'VE sometimes wondered if the stricken woman,
  Who wept in anguish by the Crucified,
Found in her mother nature, fond and human,
  No longing to be nearer while he died.

Just to have held his head upon her breast,
  And loving looks and kisses showered down ;
With burning tears, that could not be repressed,
  Scattered like jewels in his thorny crown.

Or, if this yearning asked of God too much,
  If she would be denied a care so sweet,
Surely she might, with tender, reverent touch,
  Have wiped the blood-drops trickling from his feet.